Dealing with Loneliness

By

EDEN WILSON

Table of contents

Chapter 1

Chapter 2

Chapter 3

Chapter 4

Chapter 5

Chapter 6

Chapter 7

Chapter 8

Chapter 1

Loneliness

It's important to define loneliness which is referred to as a feeling of being lonely. In this condition, patients go through a profound sense of emptiness as well as a sense of detachment from others around them, making the people they are with now meaningless.

That individual might be alone or in a large group, married or unmarried, young or old. In essence, they struggle greatly to relate to people and share experiences thereby bringing about separation from important ties. This is not the same thing as being by yourself.

Being alone does not always mean that a person is lonely because being alone can offer opportunities for renewal, recuperation, and rediscovery of important aspects of our lives. Being alone can also be beneficial at times. If you are reading this book, what are some typical signs which show that you are alone? You could be experiencing one of these signs, in my opinion.

- You feel as though other people have friends while you don't because you believe your problems are so singular that nobody else can relate to them.

- You also feel very self-conscious about everything.
- You do feel humiliated when you make a mistake.
- When in a crowd, you feel drowned out by everyone else's voices.
- You feel distant from the group despite being with them.
- You feel shy and afraid of other people.

Chapter 2

Loneliness in Relationship

Have you ever felt as though your spouse doesn't comprehend you? Even when your spouse or other close relationship is standing right beside you, the gap remains. Despite being surrounded by many people, their presence causes you to "drown" even more into solitude! People experience that manner since we are all diverse and unique. Some of the things you need to observe is that, nobody in the entire world will have the same personality, views, or experiences similar to your demands and way of life NONE! even not twins!

How could somebody complete all those requirements to satisfy each individual? In the Bible, it is said that if I attempt to remove the speck from my, I must first remove the plank from MY eye before I can do the same for my neighbor's eye.

We somehow learn to demand less from others and it eases the agony because we realize that others are not required to meet our requirements. Giving people some wiggle room results in the first step in overcoming loneliness. Keep in mind that the five individuals we spend the majority of our time with make us who we are.

If you hang around with a group of people that are constantly negative and depressed, it is not surprising that you will be depressed and alone at this time. There is no surprise that children leave their homes to avoid having bad parents or quit working with certain groups of bad companies.

The fundamental cause of loneliness is man's inability to love others.
The consequences of pain are drawn to the loneliness symptoms to the point which increases our own awareness of oneself and fosters self-preoccupation thereby making it difficult to love other people.

Chapter 3

Pain of loneliness

How does the pain of loneliness appear to reach men and women's hearts all across the world? Even celebrities who have served as the faces of millions of people, including feel unsatisfied.

Has your stomach ever ached? Who are you currently considering?
This demonstrates how selfish we are by serving just our own interests. It depicts a reality that is incredibly painful for us to live in.
Additionally, the discomfort does subside, much like a stomach ache. Now

that suicide rates are through the sky and the majority of ailments in the world today are either psychologically generated or treated in psychiatric facilities, the so-called mid-life crisis is more resembling a "young adult" problem.

The rate at which people open up for themselves has reduced drastically. People won't open up to you if you don't first open up to them, therefore neglecting to do so causes the symptoms of loneliness to appear. It is stated that in order to attract friends, one must first extend friendship to others.

Chapter 4

Love

Loneliness festers in a person's heart when they experience love, or rather when they don't. The reality that we are mostly influenced by others, specifically the five individuals we spend the majority of our time with; who have control over our future, is frightening. We are what we are now because of the people who have either loved us or have chosen not to. Others are given life by love, but the most crucial thing to keep in mind is that loving ourselves comes before loving anybody else. What you don't have, you can't offer!

If you don't love yourself, you can't love others. When you love yourself first, you create the ground or foundation upon which you love others; otherwise, what passes for love is really a baseless act of self-deception but if we have never experienced love, how can we love ourselves? We shall investigate this area in the following chapter.

Chapter 5

Learning how to love

How do I deal with loneliness in the beginning? through developing love. However, we must first investigate the paradox of love.

We get the feeling of being in an agonizing jail when we are alone. The focus is solely on ourselves when we are lonely, much like when we have stomach pain. So, in an effort to fill this need, we search for people who will show us the exact kind of love we require.

People frequently strive to please others in order to win their love. They swap favors and barter with one another while seeming to be kindhearted individuals. We must experience the affection of others since we are aware that only their love can satisfy our loneliness.

The paradox of love is that we will eventually find no solace but only a deeper despair if we try to fill the gap of our own loneliness by looking for affection from others. In other words, we will never discover the love we need if we search for it. No matter how sad it may be, a person is fundamentally self-centered when they live their lives in a way that prioritizes meeting their own wants and seeking the affection they so desire. Such an individual will never be able to truly love since he will constantly be preoccupied with himself.

A person will become beloved and will almost surely end up being liked by others if they strive to offer love rather than receive it.
We need to start caring about other people instead of just ourselves. The first step to finding love and overcoming loneliness is to start with the goal in mind, which focuses on the outcomes of the act of loving others without thinking about self-gain.
Every single individual on the planet is capable of loving in some way.

Every one of us has the capacity to shift our focus from our own wants and concerns to those of others. We can only accept the affection of others to the degree that we are prepared to offer. Making the decision to love people unconditionally is not a barter deal; rather, it is more like a donation (we don't ask for anything in return, not even a pleased ego or lessened guilt). We have failed to love when we ask others, "What have you done for me?"

Even if you can only love a little at first, you will still receive a little love in return. You will be able to develop and give forth more love, which will enable you to receive more love in return.

Chapter 6

Laws of Attraction

Have you ever wondered why some people receive the courteous, "Good Morning, Sir," treatment while others only receive "Hey Bud" or "Hey, Mac"? Now, consider for a second, besides a few billion bucks, what separates Donald Trump from a beggar? together with a few skyscrapers? The squishy interior of your skull is the solution.

You see, how you perceive yourself affects how other people respond to you. Why do you believe that people tend to evaluate a person by their appearance or a book by its cover? I know it seems unjust, yet a person will manifest or even carry out what he or she believes in their heart.

There is nothing new about the Law of Attraction; it just describes how things are. Murphy's Law makes it clear that we frequently experience the things we least want to; for example, a dropped piece of buttered toast will always land on the wrong side. I had always hoped that when I saw someone sitting in class, even as a young student, they would...I always said in my heart, "I don't know how to answer the question the teacher asked," ``Please, don't select me," the student begged, and the instructor always did. It was irrelevant.

The teacher knew I didn't know the material because she could read my mind from where I was seated, wasn't listening or didn't have a response. How does this relate to getting over loneliness?

You will feel unwelcome and be subconsciously rejected by your pals if you "project" an atmosphere of unwelcomeness. Stop behaving like an unwelcome, damp dog that just ran away from the pound.
"You find me beautiful, loveable, and wonderful company," tell yourself. It's

true that sometimes we have to remind ourselves that we are admirable, attractive, and that people enjoy being around us.
However, since we have no control over what other people may believe, this type of affirmation just tricks our minds into believing that WE ARE charming and handsome.

Chapter 7

Steps You Can Take To End Loneliness

There are several strategies to start overcoming loneliness, like making friends, taking care of yourself, or learning to feel better about yourself in general.

Make an effort to talk to someone NEW. Remind yourself frequently that the loneliness you feel is TEMPORARY and that you will get over it in due course. I'm aware that it's challenging, but you have to get moving, and the first step is generally the most difficult but crucial.

Put yourself in circumstances where you'll encounter new individuals. Take part in things that truly interest you. Connect with individuals who share your interests by joining clubs, organizations, and church groups.

QUIT listening to depressing music. OPEN YOURSELF to others. Don't expect people to confide in a closed person about their difficulties. Don't evaluate new people based on your previous interactions with senior citizens. Try to see each person you meet from a new perspective \ instead of being judgmental.

Intimate friendships typically grow over time as people learn to communicate their innermost thoughts and feelings. Don't expect people to provide too much information or hurry into close relationships. Don't limit your search to romantic partnerships. Even platonic or casual friends may be quite satisfying.

Live a wholesome life. Never overlook getting enough sleep, exercising, and eating healthfully. The absence of such items is one of the primary factors in depression, which breeds loneliness. You can better assess oneself by spending time alone.

Don't take advantage of your buddies. They'll be there for you if you ask for their sympathy and care. However, if you constantly blabber on and on about your difficulties, it gets annoying, and at worst, your buddies will amuse you.

Consider the pleasant times you've had and give thanks.

Acquire new knowledge. When you succeed at something, you'll feel confident in yourself.

It is OK to seek medical advice if you have had long-term depression. It is perfectly OK to get a prescription as depression may also be brought on by a body's lack of certain nutrients, which is easily remedied. Taking the right medicine in the proper dosage when we feel hungry and seeking food is the greatest way to fight depression and feel less lonely.

Spend some time in solitary prayer and counseling.

Chapter 8

Breaking the Cycle of Destruction

Be careful not to act heroically just because you're lonely.
You might be shocked. A subtle type of pride is self-pity. Ones who are proud take pride in their accomplishments, whereas self-pitying people take pride in their hardships.
We were made to be in relationships with one another, thus it is quite harmful to spend too much time alone.
It is an ingrained trait of people that cannot be changed. If you spent your childhood alone in a forest, it's likely that

you would communicate with plants or animals in your own language.

- The biggest concern is that these rare things can occur if someone indulges in their loneliness for too long.
- The lonely addict rejects any attempts to rekindle relationships, causing great suffering for those close to them when their attempts to assist the individual are turned down.
- They will feel more vindicated when they ultimately shout, "Look at them; I was right all along that they never cared for me at all!" when the

connections around them gradually break down.

- The addict of loneliness eventually develops an immunity to the suffering and accepts loneliness as a way of life. He's too indolent to make a change.

Finding It in the Wilderness

Here is a tale that will inspire you. What gives us genuine purpose in life when all the money in the world, the pinnacle of fame, and the height of power have been achieved?

To live, many living creatures depend on one another. If you've ever seen an aspen tree in Colorado, you might have observed that it doesn't grow in isolation. Aspens grow in groves or clusters. The aspen grows new shoots from the roots, which is the cause. It's possible that all of the trees in a small grove are linked via their roots!

The tallest California redwoods may reach heights of 300 feet. They appear to need incredibly deep roots to hold them against heavy winds. However, it has been revealed that in order to absorb as much surface water as possible, their roots are really rather shallow. And they grew widely, entwining with other redwoods in every way.

All the trees are intertwined in this fashion, supporting one another during wind and storms.
They never exist by themselves, just like the aspen. They cannot survive without one another.
A network of roots connects people as well. We grow up with friends we create because we are born into a family. We are not designed to live alone for very long. And we must support one another, just like the redwood. When

www.ingramcontent.com/pod-product-compliance
Lightning Source LLC
LaVergne TN
LVHW052114160826
845678LV00015B/3539

* 9 7 9 8 8 4 7 0 2 4 7 3 0 *